Nottinghar
Cricket(

on old picture postcards

Grenville Jennings

JOHN GUNN BATTING.

1. Rotary Photographic Co. card illustrating the First Test match at Trent Bridge in June 1899. It was between England and Australia and the result was a draw. W. Gunn, the sole Nottinghamshire representative, scored 14 and 3.

INTRODUCTION

The Golden Age of Cricket is generally recognised as having been the years between 1900 and 1914. It ran almost parallel with the appearance in Great Britain of the picture postcard (1894) and the period between 1900 and 1918 known as the Golden Age of Postcards, when Europe's postal system was swamped by the mailing of millions of cards every year.

Postcard collecting was a major hobby in the first decade of this century, with many thousands of families amassing vast numbers of cards from all over Britain and – for those with wealthy connections – the continent. Many were sent with the message *"here's another one for your collection"*, while others were bought with the intention, not of mailing them, but keeping them in the family postcard album. Specialist magazines catered for the craze, and publishers produced cards on all kinds of themes, cricket being a major one.

As Nottinghamshire were acknowledged as one of the 'big six' counties (Middlesex, Yorkshire, Lancashire, Kent and Surrey were the others) of the Edwardian period, the county's cricketers figured quite prominently on postcards by the leading publishers. Chief among these were E. Hawkins of Brighton, Evelyn Wrench of London, and the Rotary Photographic Co. of London. In addition a number of local photographers got in on the act, and there was a major series – though of inferior quality – from Gottschalk, Dreyfus & Davis in the 'Star' series. Quite the best of the photographic cards came from Brighton-based Hawkins, who ran a shop dedicated to the production of cricket photography. He issued postcards up to the beginning of the Great War, and every team that played Sussex at Hove were photographed, cards being published of each individual player plus the respective county XI. They sold at a penny each or sixpence for a set of twelve, and it cost a halfpenny postage to mail the card.

This booklet shows a fair cross-section of cricketers who appeared for the county team during the Golden Age, plus a selection of inter-war players, many of them household names.

Cricket has continued to grip the attention of the nation, with radio and television coverage and the one-day competitions giving it a more broadly-based following, but the popularity of picture postcards waned sharply after 1918, as other forms of communication improved and the postage rate doubled to a penny.

Now, though, a new generation of postcard collectors has grown up, interested in the images on pre-1939 cards, and the fascinating postcards of the Edwardian era are once again lovingly collected.

Grenville Jennings, October 1990

£3.50

Reprinted and revised
1995,1998, 2003

ISBN 0 946245 34 7

2. The original Trent Bridge Inn (T.B.I.) which was pulled down in 1884 to be replaced a year later by the existing building. The T.B.I. was associated in the very early days of cricket with William Clarke, who laid out the cricket ground in 1838 and founded the all-England eleven of cricketing professionals in 1846.

ARMS OF NOTTINGHAM

3. Trent Bridge cricket ground (and city arms) on a postcard published by Raphael Tuck and posted at Derby in November 1905.

4. 'Clumber' series card no. 217 by local publisher Hindley showing Trent Bridge about 1906.

Notts XI.

5. Wrench series postcard (no. 3373) of the 1902 county team. Led by A.O. Jones, it finished third in the Championship, winning 6 out of 20 games with 11 drawn. This was Notts' best position since 1892.

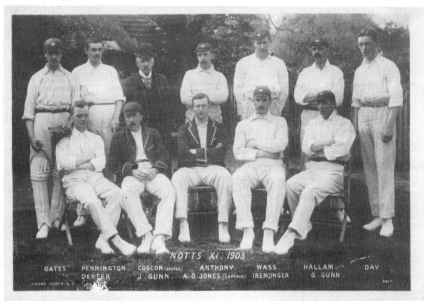

NOTTS XI. 1903

OATES   PENNINGTON   COSCON *(scorer)*   ANTHONY   WASS   HALLAM   DAY
DEXTER   J. GUNN   A.O. JONES *(captain)*   IREMONGER   G. GUNN

6. Rotary Photo card showing Notts in 1903. A notable absentee from the team group was Arthur Shrewsbury, whose suicide in May that year was a great shock to everyone. In the previous season he'd finished at the top of the first-class averages with 1,250 runs from 32 innings at an average of 50.

A. Shrewsbury

The Wrench Series. No. 1750

7. Arthur Shrewsbury (1856-1903) was alleged to be one of the greatest bad wicket players of all time, and the most famous professional of his day. He played for Notts from 1875 to 1902, scoring 26,505 runs and appearing in 23 Test matches. When W.G. Grace was asked who the best player in the country was – excluding himself – he is said to have replied *"Give me Arthur"*. Wrench series postcard no. 1750.

W. GUNN

8. William Gunn (1858-1921), a right-handed batsman of extreme elegance who made his debut for Notts in 1880, and was a stalwart of the team until 1904, scoring over 25,000 runs including 48 centuries. Gunn played in eleven Tests and as a professional footballer with Notts County earned two international caps. Card published by Giessen Bros. and posted at Bromley, Kent, in June 1903.

During the 1880's and 1890's Shrewsbury and William Gunn were without doubt two of the leading professional batsmen in England. In 1890 they added 398 for the 2nd wicket against Sussex at Trent Bridge (Gunn 198, Shrewsbury 267)

A TRIO OF GUNNS

JOHN GUNN.

9. John R. Gunn (1876-1963), brother of George, was an all-rounder who played for Notts from 1896 to 1925, scoring 24,557 runs and taking 1,242 wickets. In six Tests for England he captured 18 wickets but did nothing with the bat. After 1925, he became associated with the great Nottinghamshire benefactor Sir Julian Cahn. Postcard in the Wrench series, no. 1691.

10. Another card of **William Gunn**, this time published by Hartmann (no. 1656).

G.GUNN.

Copyright.
PHOTO BOWDEN BROS

11. George Gunn (1879-1958), nephew of William and brother of John. George became one of his county's finest opening batsmen, thriving on the fastest bowling. Between 1902 and 1932 he scored 35,208 runs, with 62 centuries, and played in thirteen Tests. In his later years he appeared regularly in the county XI with his son G.V. Gunn. Postcard by Gottschalk, Dreyfus and Davis in the 'Star' series.

J. IREMONGER.

T. WASS

12. Jimmy Iremonger (1876-1956) was a fine opening bat who scored 16,622 runs for Notts from 1897 to 1914. He played football for Nottingham Forest and won three England caps at full-back. Brother of Albert Iremonger, the famous Notts County footballer. Another Wrench postcard, no. 2939, posted in London in July 1907.

13. T.G. Wass (1873-1953). 'Topsy' Wass played from 1896 to 1920, taking in all 1,666 wickets. He formed a formidable partnership with A.W. Hallam and they bowled right through an innings many times. 'Star' series card postally used from Wimbledon in December 1907.

DAY   OATES   HARDSTAFF   WASS   ANTHONY   HALLAM
IREMONGER   C. R. MORRIS   A. O. JONES (CAPTAIN). GUNN (J.)   GUNN (G.)   COXON (SCORER)
PHOTO HAWKINS, BRIGHTON   NOTTINGHAMSHIRE.   COPYRIGH

14. Another 'Star' series card (from a photo by Hawkins of Brighton) of the 1904 or 1905 side. Notts finished fifth in the Championship, winning seven games. H. Coxon (seated end right front row) was team scorer from 1867-1923.

NOTTINGHAMSHIRE.

Simpson. Oates. Day. Wass. Hardstaff.
J. Gunn. Iremonger. J. A. Dixon. A. O. Jones. G. Gunn. Hallam.

15. J.A. Dixon, former county captain, appears on this postcard published by R. Scott & Co., Manchester, in 1905/6. Dixon played for Notts from 1882 to 1905 in 235 matches. He also played football for Notts County and England.

NOTTS COUNTY C.C. 1905.

T. OATES. G. ANTHONY. T. WASS. G. GUNN. J. HARDSTAFF. A. W. HALLAM.
J. IREMONGER. REV. H. STAUNTON. M? A. O. JONES. M? R. E. HEMINGWAY. J. GUNN.

16. Postcard publisher E.W. Morley has actually superimposed G. Anthony (back row, second from left) into this 1905 team photo. This re-touching was quite a common occurrence if the team remained constant! The original card was by E. Hamel & Co., Nottingham.

England v Australia 29th May 1905

17. The two captains, J. Darling and F.S. Jackson, return to the Pavilion on this E. Hamel card.

18. E.W. Morley card listing the teams including Notts players A.O. Jones and John Gunn. Jones scored 4 and 30, taking 2 catches. Gunn took a wicket and scored 8 runs.

NOTTS C.C.

H. Coxon (Scorer)   Day   Wass   Alletson   G. Williamson   Oates
J. Gunn   J. Iremonger   A. O. Jones   G. T. Branston   Hallam
Payton   Hardstaff   G. Gunn

19. This card, published by E. Hawkins of Brighton, heralds the arrival of two newcomers to the team, Edward Alletson and Wilfred Payton. Whilst Alletson's career for Notts finished in 1914, Payton was still playing first-class cricket for the county in 1931.

NOTTS. COUNTY XI. 1907.

H. Coxon (Scorer)   E. Alletson   J. Iremonger   A. W. Hallam   T. Oates   J. Hardstaff
T. Wass   J. Gunn   Mr. A. O. Jones   Mr. G. T. Branston
W. Payton   G. Gunn

COPYRIGHT.   SAM. KIRK, PHOTO.

20. 1907 was the year that Notts at last regained the Championship, the first time since 1889, so success was long overdue. Wass and Hallam took 145 and 133 wickets respectively, while John Gunn was the next most successful with 25. Card by Sam Kirk, Nottingham, posted from the city in September 1907.

21. Wilfred Payton (1882-1943) was a middle-order right hand bat who scored over 22,000 runs for Notts between 1905 and 1931. He was a member of both the 1907 and 1929 Championship-winning teams. Postcard by R. Henson & Co. of Pelham Street, Nottingham, in their 'Cobden' series.

22. Thomas Oates (1875-1949) first appeared for Notts in 1897, keeping wicket until 1925 with a career record of 758 caught and 235 stumped. He also appeared for W.G. Grace's London County team in 1900. Postcard by E. Hawkins.

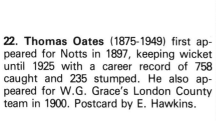

In 1907 Notts, after 21 years without success, finally made 1st place in the County Championship, without losing a match. Payton and Oates were both members of the XI, the former scoring 550 championship runs averaging 27·50. Oates, according to Wisden, was "again a very fine wicket-keeper".

HUMPHRIES.

R. A. YOUNG.

HOBBS.

F. L. FANE.

BARNES.

RHODES.

HAYES.

HARDSTAFF.

K. L. HUTCHINGS.

A. O. JONES.
captain.

FIELDER.

BRAUND.

1907

1908.

BLYTHE.

J. N. CRAWFORD.

M.C.C. AUSTRALIAN TEAM.

23. The M.C.C. touring team to Australia in 1907-8 was captained by Nottinghamshire's A.O. Jones and also included Joseph Hardstaff. Jones fell ill at the beginning of the tour, but George Gunn was in Australia – recuperating – and joined the party with great success, though Australia won the series by four games to one. An Australian published card in the 'Empire' series, posted in January 1908. *"Please excuse me not sending you this card before",* wrote Billy.

The Notts trio who toured Australia 1907-8

Mr A. O. Jones.
(Notts.)

24. A.O. Jones (1872-1914). Arthur Jones was a brilliant bat, astute captain and exceptional fielder. He scored 22,935 runs between 1892 and 1914, and for good measure took 577 catches and 333 wickets. He played in twelve Test matches for England, never doing himself full justice. Millar and Lang published this card in their 'National' series, and it was posted from London in August 1909.

25. Joseph Hardstaff (1882-1947) played in 377 matches from 1902 and 1926, scoring over 17,000 runs (including 26 centuries). He played in all five Tests in Australia in 1907-8, hitting 311 runs in 10 innings. Father of 'young' Joe, he later became a well-known umpire. Another Hawkins postcard.

26. George Gunn. His later inclusion in the 1907-8 Test series led to a century on his debut (119) followed by 74 in the second innings. Hawkins-published card.

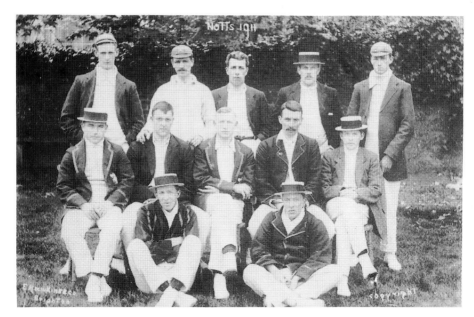

27. Another card by the prolific Brighton photographer Hawkins. Out of this county team of 1911 Iremonger and George Gunn were chosen by M.C.C. to tour Australia. Gunn was very successful, Iremonger not so, and took no part in the Tests.

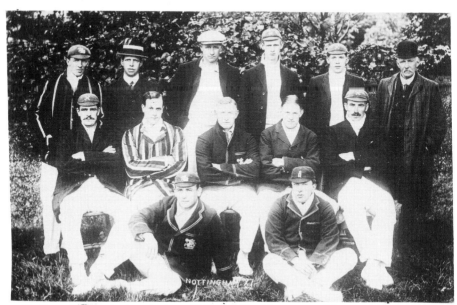

28. Posted in Nottingham in June 1912, this Hawkins postcard featured the 1912 team. This season was very badly affected by rain, to such an extent that only three out of sixteen counties were able to show a profit. Notts finished 8th in the Championship.

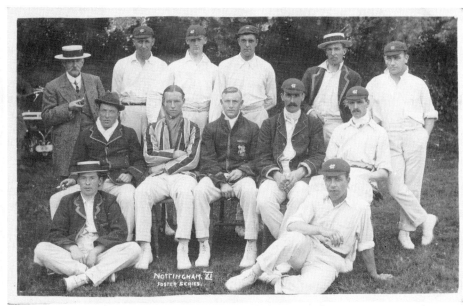

29. A young **A.W. Carr** seated next to captain A.O. Jones. Carr was a very prominent Sherborne schoolboy cricketer appearing during the school holidays as early as 1910. This team photo by Hawkins is probably of 1913 vintage.

30. **W.W. Whysall** (1887-1930). An early postcard of 'Dodger' Whysall about 1911. He played for twenty years from 1910, scoring 21,592 runs (including 51 hundreds) and winning four Test caps.

31. **William Riley** (1888-1917) was the other half of the famous last-wicket stand against Sussex in 1911 when he and Alletson added 152 runs in forty minutes, Riley scoring 10*. He was killed in Belgium in 1917 by a shell splinter. Both these last two cards are by Hawkins.

CHAMPION COUNTY 1907

32. Superb Hawki
teen matches, the
staff, Hallam and
puzzling, as they

postcard to commemorate Notts winning the County Championship in 1907. Playing nine-
n and drew three. Seven of the team – Jones, George Gunn, John Gunn, Iremonger, Hard-
:d in every match. The presence of C.R. Morris, W. Speak and Hemingway on the card is
for Notts after 1905. Hemingway was killed in action at Loos, France, in 1915.

A famous innings at Hove, May 1911

ALLETSON

A NOTTS. CRICKETERS WORLD RECORD

without parallel in Cricket History

NOTTS v SUSSEX
at Brighton 1911.

Alletson, a Notts player, was an hour making his first 50; hit his second 50 in a quarter of an hour and his last 89 in 15 minutes - After Lunch he scored 115 out of 120, in 7 overs, hitting Killick for 22 in one over, and 34 in another - His 189 out of 227 occupied him 90 minutes

33. Anonymously-published, but very scarce, postcard tells the story, in brief, of Ted Alletson's wonderful innings in May 1911 when batting number nine. He hit 189 runs in ninety minutes, sharing a last-wicket stand with W. Riley *(see no. 31)*. His driving power was so ferocious it struck fear into the hearts of Sussex fielders! John Arlott actually devoted a book to recalling this unique innings.

34. Edwin Alletson (1884-1963). Despite his glorious 189 against Sussex, this was Alletson's only century in first-class cricket. In his career from 1906 to 1914 he scored only 3,217 runs (average 18.59) and took 33 wickets (average 19.03). 'Cobden' series postcard by Henson & Co.

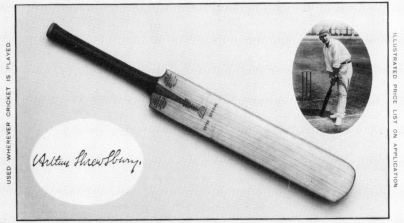

35. This card was used to advertise the sports shop on Carrington Street, Nottingham, run by the two famous Notts players, Arthur Shrewsbury and Arthur Shaw.

36. Unidentified visiting team descending the pavilion steps at Trent Bridge pre-First World War.

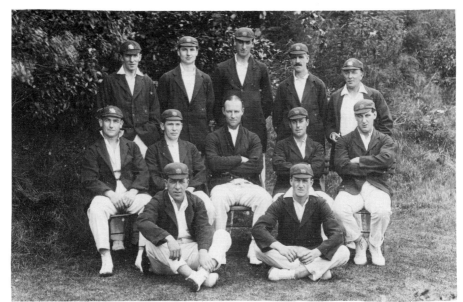

37. The Notts XI in 1920, remarkably showing only two new faces from 1914, Sam Staples (back row, second from left) and Frank Matthews (back row, centre). Notts finished seventh, playing twenty matches. Champions were Middlesex, captained by Pelham Warner in his final season. Anonymously-published card.

38. A view of Trent Bridge cricket ground in the 1920's on a postcard published by C. and A.G. Lewis (no. 3740). Under Arthur Carr's leadership, Notts once more became a very powerful team in this and the next decade, though only one Championship came their way – in 1929.

39. Sam J. Staples (1892-1950) gave good service to Notts for almost fifteen years, scoring in all 6,420 runs and taking 1,331 wickets. He appeared in three Tests for England, against South Africa in 1927-28. His younger brother Arthur also played for the county during the 1920's-30's.

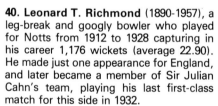

40. Leonard T. Richmond (1890-1957), a leg-break and googly bowler who played for Notts from 1912 to 1928 capturing in his career 1,176 wickets (average 22.90). He made just one appearance for England, and later became a member of Sir Julian Cahn's team, playing his last first-class match for this side in 1932.

In 1923 Notts finished 2nd to Yorkshire in the Championship, winning 15 matches and losing only 3. Richmond took 119 wickets at an average of 18·55 and Staples captured 89 at 17·91. F.C. Matthews took 115 wickets and finished 7th in the first-class bowling averages.

41. In finishing eighth in the 1921 Championship, Notts again relied heavily on players who'd begun their careers pre-war. Both Gunns were in their forties and Oates was forty-six, though as nimble as ever. Card by Douglas Studios, Alfred Street Central, Nottingham.

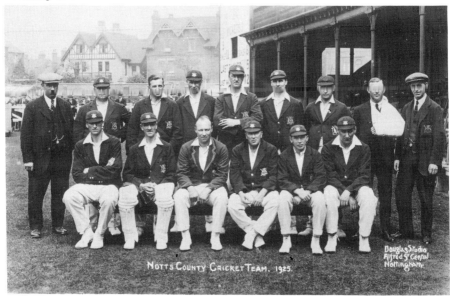

42. Though not on the team photo for 1925, this was the year that 20-year old Harold Larwood came into the eleven. From mid-June, he took 73 wickets at an average of 18.01 each. Notts won fifteen games, finishing fourth in the Championship. Another Douglas Studios card.

Two prominent members of the Notts XI's of the 1920's

43. Willis Walker (1892-1991) first appeared for the county in 1913 and was a regular until 1937, scoring 18,259 runs (average 32,37) with 31 centuries. He passed away at the age of 99, just missing another personal century.

44. W. Whysall on a card by Nias, Brighton, about 1925.

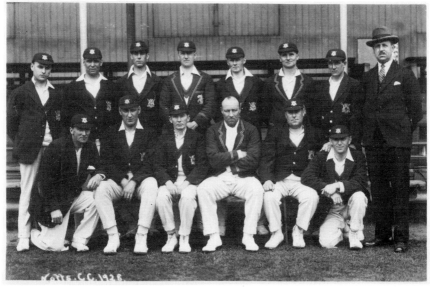

45. The County Championship of 1928 was very much a batsman's paradise, and 414 first-class centuries were scored. Seven batsmen passed a thousand runs for Notts, and eight made centuries. Whysall led the run glut with 2,573. Card by anonymous publisher, posted at Nottingham in June 1928. *"Here is a picture of the men who failed 'on the post' to add another glorious chapter to Notts cricket history",* wrote A.W. Shelton to a friend in Great Malvern.

46. Marvellous montage of the English players chosen by the selectors for the first Test at Trent Bridge in 1926. The team was led by Arthur Carr of Notts, and the two left out of the final eleven were Holmes and Sandham. Published by Douglas Studio, the card was actually postally used in 1973, when Bill wrote *"A relic of the past! Just one of my hoarded treasures!"* The match, incidentally, was washed out by rain.

47. Arthur W. Carr (1893-1963) was an inspiring, even controversial captain. He played for Notts from 1910 to 1934, leading them to the county title in 1929, and scoring 21,051 runs in his career. He led absolutely from the front, was a forceful attacking batsman and a brilliant close fielder. He in turn was dismissed from the English captaincy in 1926, was instrumental in the 'bodyline' tour of Australia in 1932-3, and was finally sacked by Notts in 1934.

48. This postcard was actually used in the montage opposite. **A.W. Carr** captained England four times in 1926 before being replaced for the fifth Test by Percy Chapman.

Arthur Carr captained the Notts XI from 1919-34, during which time they were one of the most powerful teams in the Championship. He completed 1,000 runs in a season eleven times. Of stern appearance, he had a kind and generous nature.

49. Ben Lilley (1895-1950) was for many years a deputy to the never-ageing wicket-keeper Oates, but took over behind the stumps in 1925. In a twelve-year career, he caught 657 and stumped 132 victims. No mean bat, he scored 16,496 runs with seven hundreds. No indication of who published the card, but it was probably J. Webb of Douglas Studios.

50. Charles Bowmar Harris (1907-1954) was a very good opening batsman, but numerous stories about him testify to his eccentricity. From 1932, he was a regular member of the county side, scoring 18,823 runs including 30 hundreds. With Walter Keeton, he shared in 46 century opening partnerships.

51. A fine postcard by C.F. Shaw commemorating Notts' winning of the 1929 County Championship, led by Arthur Carr. Only George Gunn and Wilfred Payton were survivors from the previous success in 1907.

52. The M.C.C. team to Australia in 1932-3, captained by Douglas Jardine, contained two Notts players in Harold Larwood and Bill Voce, whose 'leg theory' bowling provided the spark for considerable notoriety. The allegation that it had been pre-planned by Jardine and Notts captain Arthur Carr merely inflamed the situation.

53. Harold Larwood (1904-1995) is regarded as one of the fastest bowlers of all time. He took 1,427 wickets (average 17.51) from 1924-38 until injury forced his retirement.

54. William Voce (1909-1984) took 1,558 wickets (average 19.21) from 1927 to 1952, appearing in twenty-seven Tests for England. He is probably most associated with 'bodyline'. Postcard by B. & H. Ltd.

55. George Vernon Gunn (1905-1957) was the son of the famous George. G.V. succeeded as a good all-rounder from 1928 to 1950, appearing in over 250 matches. He scored 10,337 runs (average 29.36) and took 281 wickets (average 35.67). In 1931, both he and his father scored a century in the same innings against Warwickshire at Edgbaston. G.V. was 100* and father George 183 – a unique achievement. He died following a motor-cycle accident in 1957.

56. Arthur B. Wheat (1898-1973) was a capable deputy to Ben Lilley; in 91 games, he caught 152 and stumped 21 batsmen. When Lilley retired, Wheat made the wicket-keeping position his own, but the Second World War ended his county career after only a couple of seasons. Both this and the previous postcard were published by C.H.P.

Wheat and G.V. Gunn were both regular members of the Notts team in 1939 which was the last first-class season prior to the second world war. Notts finished 12th in the Championship, winning 6, losing 8 and drawing 9 of the 23 finished matches played.

---

57. Frank G. Woodhead (1912-1991) made 141 appearances for Notts from 1934 to 1950. He took 320 wickets (average 32.96). In the 1970's he was team coach, placing an emphasis on producing local talent for the county team rather than relying on 'imports' from other counties.

58. Harold J. Butler (1913-1991). Illness and injury at the wrong time robbed Butler of more than just his two England caps. He first appeared in the Notts eleven in 1933, and after the war was acknowledged as one of the fastest bowlers in England. By the time he retired in 1954, he'd taken 952 wickets at an average of 24.44. Card published by B. & H. Ltd.,

---

In 1938, Harold Larwood only bowled 103 overs for the county due to his rheumatism, so the opportunity for both Woodhead and Butler to assist Voce in the attack was there for the taking. However, Butler was taken ill with appendicitis (at the time he led the first-class averages) and an ankle injury to Woodhead limited his haul to 69 wickets. Notts finished 12th, well down the table. Winners that year were Yorkshire.

59. Joe Hardstaff Jnr. (1911-1990) was another son of a famous batsman, though 'young' Joe, with due respect to his father, was a far more accomplished player. From 1930 to 1955 he scored 31,847 runs (average 44.35) with 83 centuries and a top score of 266. His elegant strokeplay brought him 23 appearances for England with a most respectable average of 46.74.

The careers of Payton and Hardstaff spanned 51 years of county cricket, excepting the two world wars, and yet Notts only won the Championship twice in this period (1907 and 1929). While Payton played in many powerful combinations, especially in the 1920's, Hardstaff often found himself in weak teams, rooted consistently at the foot of the Championship table.

60. Wilfred Payton (1882-1943) first played for the county in 1905 though his career lasted until 1931, the year when he came out of retirement to help Notts out of a serious injury crisis.

61. 'Young' Joe Hardstaff in full flight on this anonymously-published postcard.

Sir Julien Cahn (1882-1944) was a considerable benefactor of English cricket, especially Notts, between the two wars. He ran his own cricket team, inviting many of the leading players of the time to appear for him. His original ground was on Loughborough Road, West Bridgford, though later he moved to Stanford Hall.

62. A weakened All India touring team played the Cahn XI at Loughborough Road on August 27th and 29th 1932, the powerful home XI thrashing the tourists by an innings and 26 runs. This card shows Sir Julian (right) tossing for innings.

63. Sir Julien's team photographed outside the Loughborough Road pavilion.

Sir JULIEN CAHN'S CRICKET TEAM, 1937

Equipped throughout with "Viyella" Cricket Shirts, "Viyella" Socks.

Back Row, Left to Right

R. C. Butterworth
S. D. Rhodes
C. C. Goodway
J. B. Hall
R. J. Crisp
G. F. Summers
C. R. Maxwell

Front Row, Left to Right

J. Walsh
E. G. Wolfe
B. H. Lyon
Sir Julien Cahn
D. P. B. Morkel
I. A. R. Peebles
C. S. Dempster

Seated on Ground

T. B. Reddick
H. Mudge

64. The team also toured overseas. In 1928-9 they went to Jamaica, in 1929-30 to Argentina, 1933 to North America, 1936-7 to Ceylon, and 1938-9 to New Zealand.

65. The reverse of the above card, published by the Times of Ceylon, was autographed by the team, the names indicating the calibre of the side. Many county and Test players were regulars, and included here were C.S. Dempster (Leicestershire and New Zealand), D.P. Morkel (South Africa) and I.A.R. Peebles (Middlesex and England).

66. Harold Larwood was no mean batsman; indeed, he once scored 98 runs against Australia in 1933. In his career, he scored 7,290 runs (average 19.91) with three hundreds. This postcard, published by J. Webb, Douglas Studios, shows him at the crease.